To Lisa and family~

Schooltime Reflections - Feelings 202

By

Margaret Dunajski Harde

© 2011 Margaret D. Harde
All Rights Reserved.

No part of this publication may be reproduced, stored in a retrieval system, or transmitted, in any form or by any means, electronic, mechanical, photocopying, recording, or otherwise, without the written permission of the author.

First published by Dog Ear Publishing
4010 W. 86th Street, Ste H
Indianapolis, IN 46268
www.dogearpublishing.net

dog ear
PUBLISHING

ISBN: 978-145750-495-2

This book is printed on acid-free paper.

Printed in the United States of America

DEDICATION

I am dedicating this book, <u>Schooltime Reflections - Feelings 202</u>, to my late parents, Wanda and Stanley Dunajski; my sister, Joan Celestine; my son, Karl Stanley; his children, my "grandtwins," Kayla and Zachary; my husband, Henry; my additional step-grandchildren from my melded family (Emily, Graham, Natalie and Scott); and finally, to all of my students and close friends.

Table of Contents

Dedication iii

Acknowledgments...ix

Introduction..1

Chapter 1 – Sensing a Child's Feelings 7

Chapter 2 – Being Perceptive of a Child's
      Needs..15

Chapter 3 – Recognizing the Uniqueness
      in Each Child..19

Chapter 4 – Teaching Sensitivity to Others'
      Feelings..23

Chapter 5 – Giving Proper Recognition
and Credit..31

Chapter 6 – Reinforcing the Importance
of Praise and Encouragement........................37

Chapter 7 – Building Self-Esteem 43

Chapter 8 – Using Humor to Calm a
Situation 51

Chapter 9 – Understanding the Mind-Body
Connection 57

Chapter 10 – Using Names Correctly..................61

Chapter 11 – Discovering When Feelings
Begin 67

Chapter 12 – Keeping in Mind the Importance
of Feelings in Your Career Choice.................71

Chapter 13 – Concluding Observations
and Summary...75

Acknowledgments

I would like to express my sincere appreciation to the gracious people to whom I have dedicated this book and who have served as my inspiration in the writing of <u>Schooltime Reflections – Feelings 202</u>.

To my late parents, Wanda and Stanley Dunajski who, through their genes and a warm, secure, and loving environment, gave me my foundation in life. Both of them taught me how to be caring and unselfishly loving and giving. In addition, they instilled in me the determination to value the important things in life, to make priorities, and to stick to my convictions.

My sister, Joan Celestine, who reinforced my family loyalty and taught me to face the bullies in my life (or sometimes faced them for me)! We are quite different in temperament, but we are both from the same loving foundation. This has always kept us close at heart.

My son, Karl Stanley, who is my only child from a brief first marriage, and who has taught me to take the time to stop and smell the flowers and not to lose the "child" in me. I almost lost him at birth because of severe complications, but miracles do happen. (He was born on November 30, coincidentally on the same date as his stepfather, Henry). When our eyes first met at 3:19 p.m. on the day of his birth, I knew that nothing would unlock our bond. My "Starshine" is truly one of the most thoughtful, creative, and introspective persons I have ever known. He shines when he funnels these traits in a positive path, is treated with love, and is appreciated for who he is. He also created the beautiful illustration used for the cover of this book.

My "grandtwins," Kayla and Zachary, whom I had the delight of seeing from birth and had the pleasure of taking care of one day or more a week for three years (ages one to almost four). We blissfully called it "Fridays with Nana!" I was even able to write a portion of this book when they took their afternoon naps! They are so loving and sensitive, and they radiate joy when they are encouraged to follow their hearts. I hope that, in school and in life, they will come in contact with perceptive, compassionate, and encouraging people who will respect their feelings. Perhaps reading, or having read, this book might enlighten some of their future teachers.

To my four step-grandchildren - Emily, Graham, Natalie, and Scott, who have added a new dimension and amazing happiness in my life. Moreover, I have learned that trying to understand the emotions of my entire adult family, dealing, and coping with an array of new situations is very important in bringing people together in a loving, extended family.

To the late Ed Jacobson, one of my ninth grade teachers, who nurtured the idea of my becoming an educator in the field of social studies. He was also my first principal and hired me as a seventh grade social studies teacher in the Peekskill City School District.

While I always wanted to become a teacher, I will never forget the lasting impression that Mr. Jacobson made on me. He taught me to learn how to think on my own, to accept challenges, and to enter new realms of knowledge without fear. He also taught and encouraged me to enter the world of writing openly and honestly. He was one of the best writers I have known, and his influence continues to be an important part of my life. He was one of the first to read a draft of this manuscript and in his feedback to me he said, "...I am really moved by your whole book. I think it should be read by everyone who is a teacher. You have provided so many basic needs that will eventually be such an advantage to all students – let alone teachers. It is ...based upon meaningful experiences and a foundation for anyone who wants to be a good teacher..."

A special note of appreciation to my dear friend, Wendy Arnold, for guiding me in the editing process in such a skillful and sensitive way. Wendy, also an educator, wrote in a note to me, "Thank you for giving me the pleasure of proofreading your book! What an inspiration it is!! Your "lessons" are both practical and elevating. I loved them!"

To all of my students whom I have had the pleasure to teach. I hope that I have touched the hearts and minds of the thousands of these young people who have been my students over the years in such a way so that they not only have tapped their talents but that they are, or will be, following their dreams. In addition, I wish that, in pursuing their dreams, they will be doing so in a way that will make them more responsive to the feelings of those who surround them and guide them.

I also want to acknowledge my close and caring friends who have always helped me to see the light and who have affected my life in so many ways.

Lastly, a special note of thanks to my dear husband, Henry – my "rock", my friend, my confidant, and the one who has shown me to greet each day with renewed hope. The man who has told me that I have made him more caring and sensitive than he ever thought he could be. Since my close friends know that I am "technologically challenged," they will understand that without Henry's secretarial skills (on the computer), his editorial skills, and his positive reinforcement, this book would still be written in longhand!

In conclusion, my acknowledgments are somewhat lengthy because I have always felt that you should give proper credit where credit is due! All of these influential people have been mentioned because they have directly touched my heart - MY FEELINGS - which, after all, is what this book is about.

Introduction

MY CHILDHOOD EDUCATIONAL memories and the ongoing reflections about my life are the inspirations for the title of this book. The book deals with my feelings and my understanding of these feelings while I was growing up, and later becoming a teacher in the school system of my hometown, Peekskill, New York.

My real-life stories described in the following chapters, taken from actual teaching and life experiences, are the emotional guide upon which I built my approach to teaching and interacting with students and others. In order to keep them readily in mind, I have also outlined some specific "lessons" derived from the experiences presented.

In these times, when tremendous emphasis is being placed on test scores, advanced courses, accomplishments, and other results-oriented measurements, we must never lose sight of the fact that we are always dealing with people - people who have feelings. Feelings are an important part of a person's overall character. I would encourage everyone who reads this book to take the time to recall, and make note of some of their own school experiences and how their feelings were affected – positively or negatively. I am sure that, when they do, they will be very surprised as to how many of these recalled experiences, and the related emotions, seem to remain ever crisp in their minds and hearts.

School bells traditionally start the school day; but in my case, they actually rang in the start of my life! As my mother recalled, it was from her room in the "old" Peekskill Hospital on Bay Street, in Peekskill, NY, that she remembered hearing the school bells ringing from the former Franklin Street Elementary School at 8:50 a.m. on February 24, 1943. That was the exact time she noted in her records concerning that day - the day I was born and the story of my life began! I believe this foreshadowed the importance that school and teaching would play in my life!

My childhood was a very happy part of my life. Being loved unconditionally, feeling secure and protected, all in a positive and loving home environment, was all I ever needed or wanted. I really did not have a care in the world.

I remember the details of my school days – what I wore, how and what I felt, and how I internalized it all. I am going to concentrate on my early years in the educational environment since those early feelings, both affirmative and negative, are what helped make me the teacher I am today. Throughout this book, I will refer to the actual teachers' names as Ms "A." or Mr. "B.", etc. in alphabetical order.

I believe that I was destined and blessed to become a teacher. I have always made it a point to tell my students that they will spend a third of their lives sleeping, a third with family and friends, and a third pursuing their careers. So, with that in mind, they should try to seek careers in which they will love what they do! I did, and I still do!

Starting with good and honest feelings about what we are seeking to become sets the foundation for a successful and distinguished career. That career can soar because at the heart of it is what we hold dear – our roots and our feelings.

While schooling and training are important, college does not really prepare us for the true essence of what it takes to be excellent educators. It is, I believe, something that is ingrained in us – something that we are born with and/or learn along the path we take toward our goal of "teacherhood." Moreover, I think these attributes stay with us all of our lives.

What is at the core of our desire to be excellent teachers may seem obvious, but it can sometimes be overshadowed by curriculum concerns, student assessments, and educational politics. That core is also tempered by what we experience, our introspective intelligence, our deepest thoughts, the emotions we express, and the sensations to which we respond. Simply put, our <u>feelings!</u> Our feelings leave an indelible mark on our hearts and souls unlike other things we learn like a plane geometry theorem or the names of the nations in the Iroquois Confederacy. Our feelings are all that is left when we sometimes forget the academic specifics and even the concepts of what we have learned.

Assuming that most teachers in recent years have taken some courses dealing with "affective education," I took a step up from the introductory title designation of "101" – to a more advanced "202." Another reason for choosing "202" for part of my book's title is that my classroom number in June 2003, the year I retired from being a full-time teacher in the Peekskill Middle School, was "202"!

Although I have retired from full-time teaching, education will always be in my blood. That is why I have continued to be connected with education by mentoring, tutoring, reading stories to a first grade class whose teacher was a student of mine in the late 1960's, conducting classes for the Bright Beginnings literacy program which teaches parents-to-be about the importance of reading with their children, and supervising student teachers through a local university.

By the way, the day I made the decision to retire from full-time teaching, the clock in my classroom stopped, ironically, at 8:50 a.m.! A coincidence? My husband told me that he thought it was a reassuring sign that I was making the right decision and that retirement symbolized a "re-birth" for me.

When I reflected on the idea of a symbolic "rebirth", I realized that we are born with an array of feeling sensors as we enter this world. Hopefully, family love and security greet us at our births. Life happens, and then we will eventually leave the world taking with us the feelings we have accrued. I also believe that as we do depart, the mosaic of our emotions will be the last to leave us. Reflecting on, and understanding the importance of our feelings – were the main reasons that I wrote this book.

My wish is that this book will serve as a primer for present and future teachers by presenting certain "lessons" of which they should be aware and that I believe, for the most part, colleges may not teach them. I further hope that, through the sharing of my true-life "lessons" and experiences, presented in a somewhat chronological format, I will accomplish my goal to inspire, encourage, and help teachers, as well as others, to engage in continuing self-evaluation and to make any necessary adjustments in their attitudes or in their approaches to life, so they can be at their very best. Because at the heart of life's journey is that which we hold most dear - OUR FEELINGS.

CHAPTER 1

Sensing a Child's Feelings

WHEN I WAS very young, I really liked telling stories from books to the children in my neighborhood. Although it was still a few years before I went to school, I loved to mesmerize my "captive" audience with the stories as the children sat on the steps of my front "stoop" outside the four-family apartment house we lived in on Washington Street. I continued this activity throughout my pre-school years with a passion that continues even to this present day!

In the fall of 1948, I attended kindergarten at the former Franklin Street Elementary School. Almost every day, in the late morning, Ms A. would stop the class to take a twenty-minute break - perhaps to smoke a cigarette. At this time, Ms A. asked me to "read" a story to the rest of the class. I selected a book and "told" the story to the class as I showed them the book's colorful illustrations. I felt very comfortable doing this, especially since the other students, my peers, gathered around me, by the class piano, and wanted me to "read" the story to them. Our school custodian dropped by during this break to check in on us to see that everything was all right. This continued until the spring.

In the spring, Ms A. was planning to put on a school play in the auditorium for our families and friends. The play was going to be based upon one of her favorite books. One day she called Jeffrey, another student, and me over to the sink area near the entrance to our classroom. She had _The Golden Egg Book_, written by Margaret Wise Brown and illustrated by Leonard Weisgard (A Golden Book, Copyright in 1947), held tightly in her hand. The book was about spring, and the book's cover was adorned in bright pastel colors with eggs and a bunny. The theme of the book dealt with not being alone. I did not know it then, but Jeffrey and I were going to compete for the part of the "narrator" in the play.

Jeffrey was the first one instructed to read a passage from the book. As usual, he rose to the occasion. Jeffrey, who went on to become a lawyer in the1970's, spoke distinctly and at a melodiously rapid rate. Even I was impressed!

Ms A. then handed the book to me. I started to "read." After about thirty seconds of my articulate "reading," the teacher, who had been briefly distracted by a noise in the classroom, looked back at me with a scowling face and, in a harsh tone, asked me to point to the place where I was reading. I nervously pointed to the general area of the words.

Ms A. seemed very agitated and said, in a loud voice, so all the class could hear, "You don't know how to read, Marjorie!"

First of all, my name is not Marjorie. My nickname is Margie. My birth name is Margaret. The name Marjorie reminded me of that new (at that time) orange spread called margarine – ugh! Besides, my mother always used butter as a spread.

Secondly, I really thought "reading" was looking at the pictures or illustrations and then telling the story in my own words! I was astonished! Had I not been "reading" the whole year? What was the teacher thinking? Did she feel that I had played a trick on her? I was an innocent five-year-old – to me what I was doing the whole time was "reading"! I was very surprised at the teacher's new stance – but not as surprised as Ms A. was!

Ms A. was now flustered. Was it because she was embarrassed? I do not know, but in a very firm tone, she said that I could be the little girl in the play. I really would have preferred to be the doll, but Andrea had already been given the part of the little doll. Jeffrey, of course, was given the part of the narrator, and he would read the story as the rest of the class pantomimed it.

I do not remember the details of the play, nor do I remember the feelings I had on the day we performed it. What I do remember clearly is how "low" and hurt the teacher made me feel during the preliminary tryouts for the roles in the play. These feelings stayed with me through the following months.

For the rest of the year, Ms A. gave me a tambourine to play in the class band. I always longed to play the cymbals, even if only occasionally, because the tambourine made my thumb sore. In addition, whenever we played trains, the "cars" of which were made of old orange crates and put in a row near the center of the classroom, Bruce, another student, was always selected to be the conductor. He got the chance to "punch" our tickets during playtime. I really wanted a chance to be the conductor too!

In my heart, I felt that Ms A. was doing these things because she, in fact, did not like me. I attributed this "unkindness" to the incident involved with the play tryouts.

I felt this way, and I now think that these feelings could even have given me a reason for not wanting to go to school. In reality, however, I was the only child in my class that had perfect attendance at the end of the school year!

One June afternoon, Ms A. came over to our house and rang the doorbell. My mother greeted her as I peeked around the door at the top of the stairs in our apartment. Ms A. gave my mother a package and told her it was a present for me because of my perfect attendance record. The present was a nurse's kit. During her visit, Ms A. also told my mother that I was the most polite child she had ever taught! I felt proud and happy for myself as well as for my parents. It was by their example that they taught me to be kind and considerate to others. As I look back, it was really a compliment to them. I still wonder how Ms A. could really recognize politeness in a young child's life – a trait which she did not appear to practice in her own life.

To my surprise, when I was in the third grade and my older sister, Joan, was in the sixth grade, Ms A. came back into my life again in a unique way.

At the end of the school year, there was the school's annual amateur hour show. Joan and I dressed up like a bride and groom and sang a song. Joan was the groom and I was the bride. In the last verse of the song that we were performing on stage, I threw the bride's bouquet out into the audience. It was a beautiful, multi-colored arrangement that was made up of flowers from our garden and was encircled by a dainty doily. To my chagrin, Ms A. caught the bouquet!

At that moment, I wondered if Ms A. remembered, or even cared, how she had wounded my feelings and lowered my self-esteem by what she had said, in her tactless tone, in front of the whole class that spring morning three years before. Ironically, I thought, was the bouquet she caught a symbol of my subconscious state of forgiveness for her inappropriate behavior?

> LESSON - If you make a mistake, no matter what it is, or hurt someone's feelings in any way, admit to it humbly. If you do, you will touch that person's heart, no matter what their age.

CHAPTER 2

Being Perceptive to a Child's Needs

MY FIRST GRADE teacher, Ms B., rarely smiled and lacked any noticeable enthusiasm. I never knew if she really liked me or just noticed something unique about me and thought she could make use of a talent she saw in me. I will explain.

A little boy had come to the United States from Italy during the school year. Back then, there were no teachers' aides or English as Second Language (ESL) classes. Ms B. asked me to sit at a table with him every day and try to teach him some "English." She must have heard that I used to "read" stories to the children when I was in kindergarten and that I had the necessary "child leadership" skills to keep the class in order. In addition, by this time, I could really read!

I was ecstatic! The "teacher" in me came out. I began to teach him some "American" words that I knew and could pronounce correctly. I talked with the boy, guided him, read to him, and, I hoped, made him feel generally more comfortable about being in the U.S.A. His smiles and positive reinforcement of my efforts, shown by his gestures and words, fed the seed that would someday help to make me a "real" teacher.

However, during my "teacher" time, I was away from the class, and I missed the full period phonics lessons that would have helped me understand the correct pronunciation of letters and words, then and in the future.

As that year progressed, I remember telling the teacher that I felt ill sometimes and, on occasion, I recall going to the nurse to get out of the class. Maybe it was because I was afraid of making a mistake in a new phonics lesson that I did not understand. Whatever the reason, I felt no true caring or warmth from the teacher. This, plus the teacher's way of doing other class activities in a really uncreative way, made my year in the first grade unmemorable, except for my time "teaching" the young boy.

Inadvertently, the lack of the necessary phonics foundation knowledge I really needed to pronounce words correctly has lasted throughout my life in one way or another. As a result, I had, and sometimes still do have, a lack of confidence in correctly pronouncing some new or challenging words. When I mispronounce words or even when I make up new words, some people call them my "Margieisms." My husband says it is endearing.

Other than the initial thrill I felt for having been chosen to teach the young boy from Italy, I resented that I was being left out of the classroom dynamics. I wondered if Ms B. thought she just could not deal with him as a part of the class, or that she did not have the time to help him, and, therefore, used me to fill the "gap."

LESSON - Behave in a genuine warm and caring way toward all of your students. Ultimately, everyone needs to feel that he or she is special in some way and not just being "used" to fill a gap. Celebrate their uniqueness by making sure they know you consider them to be special. Be perceptive to their needs as you tap their talents.

Chapter 3

Recognizing the Uniqueness in Each Child

IT WAS A bright, sunny, and cold morning as I walked to school. It was early February and I knew that a noteworthy date for me would soon be coming up on the calendar.

Ms C., my second grade teacher, approached me in class. She pointed to a big calendar on which she had noted the famous holiday celebrations that would occur in February. Then she led me over to another large blank calendar and instructed me to circle the dates of the holiday celebrations that were scheduled in February.

She told me to place the completed calendar on an easel she had in the front of the classroom.

I neatly circled the "special" days after carefully studying the reference calendar. I remember that it was a very pleasant experience because I especially loved the month of February and always looked forward to the special holidays, as well as the changing of the seasons.

When I finished my task, I put the completed calendar on the easel. Ms C. then asked me to tell the class about the "special" days I had circled and why they were important.

I began by telling the class that February 12 was Abraham Lincoln's birthday (I always liked him because he came from a poor family). I also circled February 14 for Valentine's Day. Ms C. had a special Valentine's mailbox in the back of the room and reminded the class that we would be putting our special Valentines in that box in just a couple of weeks.

The next important day I had circled was February 22 – George Washington's birthday (I always liked him, too, because he was our first President and looked so dignified and gentlemanly).

At that point, the teacher noticed, obviously much to her dismay, that I had one more day in February circled, about which I still had to tell the class. However, before I had a chance to continue, she stopped me to ask why I had also marked February 24 as a special holiday. I responded by answering the question, somewhat humbly and quietly telling the teacher and the class that the twenty-fourth was my birthday! I added that I was going to be eight years old on that day. To my chagrin, Ms C. began to laugh and, covered her mouth with her hands. She replied rather abruptly by saying, "That is not a special holiday!" She then asked me to be seated. I felt somewhat embarrassed, confused and terribly let down. As I look back now, Ms C. seemed kind in other ways, but on this day – February 1, 1951, my heart was saddened. To me, my birthday was just as important as the rest of those other "special" days that I had circled on the calendar.

Was there no other way that Ms C. could have let a little girl know that her birthday was also significant? Perhaps she could have asked the other children in the class if anyone else celebrated his/her birthday in February or maybe she could have made a simple statement about an individual's birthday also being very important.

At this point, the class was quiet. The easel with the calendar I had been showing the class was put back in the corner, and we then went on to another activity.

<u>LESSON</u> - Recognize and be sensitive to each child's understanding and interpretation of what is truly important or special to him/her.

Chapter 4

Teaching Sensitivity to Others' Feelings

IN THE THIRD grade, Ms D. would read a chapter of <u>The Box Car Children</u> by Gertrude Chandler Warren every day after we returned from lunch. I looked forward to that story because it was about children who were being resourceful and imaginative in an adventurous environment. That, coupled with the teacher's timing by reading it after lunch, made the book a hit with the whole class.

I remember how Ms D. taught. She mostly used a cooperative approach. However, it seemed that she did not recognize individual achievements with the same importance.

The seats in Ms D.'s classroom were arranged in two columns of three desks put together in a row with a big center aisle. I sat on the left side facing the teacher; a boy was in the middle; and another girl was on the other end. Ms D. had placed green striped scarves across each set of three desks for decoration. During the day, we would fold the scarf and put it neatly away. At the end of the day, Ms D. put all the scarves back on the desks.

Ms D. indicated that she would like it if each of us were to bring in a plant to put on our desk. I was the only one of our group who remembered and brought in a plant! It was a sturdy snake plant that was in a shiny ceramic container. Snake plants are strong, sturdy, and shiny – like its owner (my mother told me that!).

Since we had only one plant for the three of us, each night before leaving school, the teacher, after putting the scarf on the desk trio, placed my snake plant on the center desk. Every morning I would come in and slowly and carefully move the plant over to my desk because, in some way, I wanted to show ownership. Also, since I was the only one taking care of my plant, I really felt that it belonged on my desk.

While I thought I understood that Ms D. probably wanted to promote, or at least demonstrate, the concept of sharing, I believe she missed a great teaching opportunity because she did not take the time to explain that to us. If she had done so, we would all have understood and shared the plant. She also left other issues open, such as not reminding the other two students about their responsibility to bring in their own plants.

Ms D. missed another very good teaching opportunity during that school year. It occurred at the time the school nurse was doing her routine yearly medical procedure that involved checking each student's hair for lice. We were very concerned because there was a "rumored" case of head lice in the school. Then it happened! A girl came back to our class with a white salve in her hair. Everyone began to whisper about the girl and that she could possibly have head lice.

Perhaps because I was brought up to be "very clean" about myself and my surroundings, I got scared and said something to the effect that I did not want to stand near the girl with the salve in her hair because I thought she had "bugs."

Ms D. overheard what I had said and briefly scolded me and the others around me, but she did not give us any other information about why we were wrong to act the way we did and why I was wrong to say what I did. She then went on to punish us by putting me, and the others she had scolded, in a dark coatroom for about twenty minutes. After the time was up, we were told to come out of the closet and to take our seats. I felt awful and I was very embarrassed about my actions and the whole situation that day.

When I got home that afternoon, I told my mother what had happened. She sat me down and gently explained to me that it was important to be sensitive and empathetic to other peoples' feelings. She also emphasized that, if I were afraid of or did not know or understand something that was going on, I should seek out a concerned adult – in this case the teacher - and tell or ask him/her about what was bothering me.

Ms D. had missed a "golden" opportunity to discuss the thought of not hurting anyone's feelings by what was being said or how one acted. I was very fortunate that my mother was the one to explain that to me.

Because of this experience and the lesson that should have been taught in class, I felt this was so important that, through my many years of being a teacher, I always had the words, "Don't hurt anyone on the inside or the outside," on a poster in my classroom and referred to it when appropriate. (Those words are from a statement that I remembered from a continuing education course.)

LESSON - Be sure not to miss any "golden" opportunities to teach about responsibility, empathy, and sensitivity to the feelings of others. These are lessons that need to be taught, and ones that may, or may not, be taught at home. They are a significant part of an education that you will carry with you and share throughout your life.

Addendum: I guess Ms D. forgave me for my insensitivity because she gave me an opportunity I will never forget! I was chosen to read the well-known poem, *The Night Before Christmas*, published in 1949 by Whitman Publishing Co. and attributed to Clement Clarke Moore. As I read the story, my classmates silently acted out their parts. I was the only one to speak! We performed before the entire school as well as parents, grandparents, etc. Ms D. tapped my talents for "reading stories" and speaking articulately – and oh! – did I feel special!

I recall wearing a red taffeta dress with a lace bodice that day and sitting in a rocking chair on stage. I also wore a special gold heart locket with my initial "M" on it that my father had given to my mother when I was born. To this day, I always have a special warm feeling whenever I wear it. (Incidentally, my "grandtwins" love looking at the pictures inside and clicking it open and shut.) Now I usually wear it with what I consider to be my most valuable piece of jewelry – a small ring that my father carved for me out of a peach pit. I was four years old and was sick with the measles when he gave it to me with the intent to cheer me up. This very unusual ring is so precious to me because of the tender love I feel he put into making it. My "grandtwins" love seeing it and putting their fingers in it.

It is uncanny that I seem to remember what I have worn on most of the memorable events in my life that have involved intense feelings. This unusual ability, coupled with my parents having taught me to dress appropriately for all occasions, a trait I apparently share with my late grandfather,

Walenty Zalewski, has stayed with me throughout my life.

I remember the day of that Christmas play as if it were yesterday. When the play was over, Ms D. gave me the book I had read from as a gift. I still have that meaningful book, and every year at Christmas time either his Nana or I would the read the story to my son as he was growing up, and now I read it to his children.

CHAPTER 5

Giving Proper Recognition and Credit

AS A TEACHER, I always taught my students to put their names on every piece of work that they completed so that they would be recognized and receive the proper credit due them for what they had done. As an example, I told them that the adventures of Christopher Columbus are written about in every history book regarding the discovery of America. This is done not only to mark his discoveries, but each account also gives him credit for the forethought he had to keep a detailed journal of his adventures. On the other hand, the Vikings are considered by some to be truly the "first" to discover the New World. However, they apparently did not leave any real, formal documentation, or other written evidence of their discoveries or other activities. Because of this, the extent and "validity" of their experiences has always been questioned.

The giving of proper credit had a real impact in my life as well. When I was in the third grade, another student and I had the same initials – M. D. During a classroom activity in which we had used alphabet stencils, we had to stencil and cut out our initials and then paste them on our booklet-type portfolios. While the other M.D. was a friend of mine, I thought, she cut things out more sloppily than I did. Not that she did it on purpose; I just think she was born without the "neatnik" or the "striving for perfection" genes that I had.

One day, when I was absent from school, the teacher told the students to take their portfolio covers home. When I returned to class the next day, I noticed that <u>my</u> "M.D." portfolio cover was missing. I was upset, and I talked to the other girl about it. Although she did not seem to understand why it really mattered so much to me, she did bring in my "M.D." portfolio cover the next day and returned it to me. She then took home her own portfolio, the one with the "M.D." she had cut out and pasted.

What also troubled me was the fact that the teacher did not seem to understand why I was bothered about the other girl taking my "M. D." portfolio cover. Even though the teacher knew that I was upset, she was insensitive to my feelings and just brushed them off.

Another incident concerning work I had done, but for which I was not given proper credit, happened in the fourth grade. This time, however, the situation was coupled with an issue involving a class "bully." Our librarian, Ms E., came up with an idea to celebrate "Library Week." I used to love the way she read stories. She was very articulate, and she pronounced some letters with a certain lilting "sparkle" in her voice.

Each student was to draw a picture, using mostly stick figures, which depicted a fact about the library or a library rule. An example of a library rule would be, "Don't dog-ear pages – use a bookmark instead." At the conclusion of this project, we were going to present our drawings to the school in an assembly.

When the day of our school presentation arrived, we all stood in line in the small auditorium waiting for our turn. Ms E. waited with us. Each child was going to be called up to go on stage. Our fourth grade teacher, Ms F., guided each student to pick up his/her completed illustration. We were told when to go on stage and to hold the picture so that the librarian could read the fact or rule as we showed our drawings to the audience.

Just before we were to begin, the class "bully" pushed in line ahead of me. I wanted to say something, but I felt it was too late to get the teacher's attention. As a result, the "bully" grabbed my tidy drawing and took the credit for it. I walked up to the stage and took his drawing (which had been under mine) from the pile and with a sad heart, held it up to the audience as the teacher read the library fact that was illustrated on it. When she was finished, I went down the steps at the other end of the stage with my head down and my heart wounded.

After our short presentation was over, I began to feel the tears welling up in my eyes. I approached my teacher and the librarian. When I was in front of them, I started talking to explain to them what had taken place. However, they did not really notice me as they were distracted by trying to organize the children to go back to their classrooms. When they finally did pay a little attention to me, I was so emotionally frustrated that I finally said, "Nothing is wrong." The teachers in charge accepted that comment and did not probe any further. Even though this incident continued to bother me, I let the issue fade.

Looking back, I wish that my teacher and/or the librarian were more perceptive as they looked into my unhappy eyes. Once again, my feelings were crushed and nothing was done by the teachers to let me know that what was done to me was wrong. Furthermore, no action was ever taken to correct the situation or punish the "bully."

<u>LESSON</u> - There is a two-fold lesson to be learned from these experiences. First, be perceptive enough to take whatever steps are necessary to make sure that each student gets credit for his or her own work. Any work that will be displayed to others is always special to the author. Even in a cooperative learning situation, individual differences must be preserved and unique talents celebrated. No matter how small the project or deed accomplished, make sure to recognize the individual student and give the appropriate credit where and when such credit is due.

Secondly, "emotional" and/or physical school bullies must be properly dealt with and the problems they cause must be addressed. When I taught in the Middle School, I told the students that I was on "bully patrol" and was there to help them should any problems arise. I also had that poster in my classroom that proclaimed, "Don't hurt anyone on the inside or the outside."

By creating a "safe" environment in my classroom, students openly came to me concerning "bully" issues or other situations where they felt hurt or compromised. As I think we know, bullies want power and sometimes have a following. Those identified as bullies, as well as those who follow along with them, have to be dealt with properly. Those who have been victimized also need to be coached so that they will understand the situation and will not continue to become "easy" targets. By taking such actions, in most cases, "bully" situations can be nipped in the bud!

Chapter 6

Reinforcing The Importance of Praise and Encouragement

THE TWO SITUATIONS described in this chapter show why it is essential to reinforce positive feelings.

In fifth grade, I was becoming a young lady. My self-esteem was positively bolstered when my fifth grade teacher, Ms G., made me her classroom assistant. I not only answered the phone on her desk when it rang, but I was also the note messenger. For doing a good job at these tasks, she praised me with kind words and positive expressions.

At that time, Ms G. was serving in dual roles at the school. She was the Acting Principal as well as a classroom teacher. Her delegation of power to me made me feel very important. The following year, my self-esteem also had a positive boost.

In the sixth grade, I had my first male teacher. As we were coming to the end of the school year, I had an idea to get a few of my friends together and create a class newspaper. The result of our efforts was a two-page typed newspaper with illustrations. Copies of the newspaper were made using carbon paper! Mr. H. praised each of us for what we had accomplished on our own outside of school. This praise was also a self-esteem booster. This constructive experience also motivated me to try out for a position on my junior high school's newspaper editorial staff when I was in the ninth grade.

I have always remembered the feeling of self-worth these confidence boosters gave me. I continued to keep them in mind during my later school years. By remembering the positive feelings these experiences gave me, I have made use of similar techniques in my own classrooms when I taught seventh and eighth grade students.

Because my fifth grade experience was so important to me, I thought how necessary it might be for my seventh and eighth grade students, who may not have had the chance to take on some responsibility outside of school, to have an opportunity in the classroom. I thought that by having classroom-related "jobs," they could get some power and respect from their classmates and their teacher. I came up with the idea of having certain "jobs" in the classroom that not only helped me with some minor tasks, but which also had meaning and usefulness in the everyday operation and maintenance of our classroom and learning environment.

Every month, in each of my classes, I asked for volunteers for the following positions: the Secretary – a messenger who brought notes where needed and helped to "stamp" the homework after I had checked it; the Electrical Engineer – the person who turned the lights off and on and helped me with the set-up of the overhead projector and videos; the Distributor – the one who passed out written materials and books; the Botanist – the student who watered and tended to the classroom plants; and the Maintenance Engineer – the person who helped to wash down the blackboards and clean erasers. By asking for volunteers and by rotating the "jobs" each month, everyone was given an opportunity throughout the year to participate actively and be responsible for an activity of their own choosing. To reinforce their participation, at the end of each month, I gave each of the helping students a certificate of recognition and thanks. I never had a shortage of volunteers to take on these classroom "jobs" as students enjoyed participating and they appeared to get a better feeling of self-worth.

My sixth grade experience with the classroom newspaper eventually did lead to a position on the editorial staff of my junior high school's newspaper. I also brought that experience to my classes, when possible, in the form of a student newsletter or in the students' participation in writing essays or papers for local organizations such as the Elks Club, Daughters of the American Revolution, or the Lincoln Society.

> <u>LESSON</u> - Praise and encourage students for taking on useful activities that are beyond the required academics, both inside and outside of the classroom. Such self-esteem boosters will always stay with a child. This praise and encouragement will help them

rise to other occasions through their memories of that "special" feeling and it just might help sow the seeds for their success in future academic or occupational endeavors.

Chapter 7

Building Self-Esteem

WHEN I ENTERED Drum Hill Junior High School in the fall of 1955, I felt that a new chapter in my life was about to begin. I was a twelve-year-old girl who was very impressionable as well as socially and academically minded. I worked very hard and was able to achieve an "A" average. I liked all of my classes – with one exception – math class! In retrospect, I do not think that this particular teacher, Ms I., really loved her life's career. I recall her as a loner and a negative-type person who did not smile very much.

Ms I. was a short woman with white hair, and she wore white blouses almost every day. She also wore a dangling charm bracelet that made horrible, annoying, and clanking noises when she wrote on the blackboard. Those sounds drove me, as well as some of the other students in the class, crazy!

Another thing I noticed about Ms I. was that she seemed to favor one cute girl. Coincidentally, the girl wore white sweater sets to school almost every day. I was friendly with her and, on occasion, even went over to her home after school. Everyone I knew wanted to be like her. She was cute, petite and, of course, the teacher's pet!

My sister also had Ms I. three years prior to my being in her class. My sister just happened to be a "whiz" in math and proved this when she went on to win Business Math and Accounting awards in high school.

I had always considered myself to be a very good math student. I did my homework all the time, paid attention in class, and tried do my best at all times. Overall, I did well in math class and continued to show my math skills in subsequent Regents math courses in high school.

Remember, we are talking about seventh grade. One's self-esteem and self-image can be so fragile – particularly at this age.

I sat near the back of the room in Ms I.'s class, and she rarely called on me. However, when she did ask for my participation, I, naturally, had to see "Murphy's Law" come into the light! For whatever reason, most of the time I either had the wrong answer to a problem, I did not understand what I was being asked to do, or I had to deal with solving a word-problem. Word problems were, and still are, sort of a weak spot with me. When I did not answer a question correctly, and/or when she was aware that I did not understand a problem, she invariably said to me, "You are nothing like your sister!" I would then feel totally demoralized and "scrunch" nervously in my seat. I knew I was not my sister - I was me!

By March, with three quarters of the school year gone, my math skills had significantly progressed to the point where I attained a solid "A" average in Ms I.'s class. I accomplished this in spite of her put-downs. During that year, my self-confidence improved, and my self-esteem triumphed over her demeaning comments. I believe that this happened because my home atmosphere and the environment in my other classes and school activities were so much more positive.

One other incident involving my self-esteem and self-confidence stands out concerning Ms I.'s math class. It just so happened that the Lenten season in the Roman Catholic Church had recently begun, and, as was the custom, I had to "give up" something for Lent. I had decided to give up chewing gum.

One day, Ms I. stopped what she was saying to the class and curtly told me to "get rid of the chewing gum." I was rather taken back that Ms I. would stop the class to say that to me. However, for the first time, I looked up at Ms I., and answered assuredly and resolutely (but not in an insolent or "smarty-pants" tone), "Ms I., I am not chewing gum. Even if I wanted to, I could not, because I have given it up for Lent!"

Ms I. just stood there silently and appeared not to have a reply to my statement. She simply turned around, went back to her desk, and continued with the class. I thought that I had handled the situation respectfully and my self-worth felt recharged.

The next year, as an eighth grader, my developing self-esteem had a significant boost when I was able to join an after-school activity called, "The Junior Miss Club." It was mainly a social club, but it had other bonuses for me as well. The significance of the positive social experiences (picnics, dinners, etc.) reinforced the building of my pride and self-esteem. Even now, I fondly remember those happy days as a young girl and how I could talk with the other members of the club about the opportunities, activities, and the common concerns we shared as eighth grade girls.

When I was hired to be a teacher in the same Jr. High School that I had attended, I became aware that the club that had been such a good influence on me was no longer in existence. However, the person who had been the past sponsor of the club was still at the school and was now my colleague. I asked her if I could try my hand at establishing a similar after-school activity. Because of the positive impact the club had in my life, I really wanted to offer the current students a similar positive experience in a safe environment. I also called it "The Junior Miss Club," although, if it were instituted today, a much "cooler" name would probably be chosen!

Under my leadership, the club was not just a social gathering place, as I also introduced a community service component. As an example, we went to the local orphanage and conducted Christmas parties for the young children who were in residence there. In addition, the club was also a place where we discussed the problems, concerns, and challenges of these young teenage girls growing up at that time.

I was able to continue my "Junior Miss Club" for just a few years. However, I am still in contact with several of my former seventh and eighth grade students who were club members. While they are now past middle age, they tell me that they still recall, as I do, the meaningful, positive, and worthwhile experiences and support the club provided as well as the lasting influence it has had in their lives.

Throughout my years of full-time teaching, I continued to have informal small group and one-to-one talks as well as class-time discussions, when appropriate. We talked about and integrated current topics that ranged from bullying and other school-related topics to friendship problems. I also incorporated the importance of community service into my class activities. We participated in such projects as helping with the restoration of the Statue of Liberty, the "Hands Across America" program which dealt with the problems of the homeless and hungry in our country, and activities that were designed to teach them the significance of patriotic holidays such as Memorial Day and Veterans Day, to name a few. These sessions and projects became a welcome, necessary, positive, and affective avenue that was open to all my students. It was very important to me that I continued to be there for them as a facilitator, sounding board, listener, and guide in their young years, in addition to being their academic teacher.

LESSON - Do not compare your students with others (especially other family members) or use language or tones that could put them down or demean them. Some students might go into their "cocoons" and never come out again because you have helped to "wreck" their budding self-esteem and/or self-confidence by thoughtless, negative remarks or approaches.

Be there in emotionally positive ways for the self-esteem and growth of your students.

Use opportunities, both formal and informal, to guide them in learning to respect themselves and others. Never underestimate the significance that your guidance and understanding has in their lives.

As an added reflection, it is important to recognize that students may not like every teacher they will encounter, or think of them as role models, for a number of reasons. However, the way a student feels about certain teachers during his/her time in school should not stand in the way of that student achieving his/her long-range goals.

Chapter 8

Using Humor to Calm a Situation

WHEN I WAS a student in the eighth grade, and later, as a teacher, when I taught eighth grade students, I experienced a few situations which were really handled well and with humor. I would like to share these experiences with you to show how negative feelings can be spared and positive results achieved.

At the time when I was a student in the mid-1950's, hair "do's" with body waves or permanents were "in." Straight hair was "out." One afternoon, my mother decided that she was going to give me a permanent. I clearly remember being so tired from the day's activities in school that we thought we would "cut short" the instructions on the box and omit some of the listed steps. One of the steps that we decided to skip was the "neutralizer" – which was usually the final step.

Well, what we did not even think might happen, happened! I woke up the next morning with an "Afro" (a hairstyle not even invented yet)! It was not me, and I did not know what to do. I probably thought it looked a lot worse than it really was, but then everything that goes wrong seems to be magnified when you are a teenager.

Since I had a perfect attendance record, and I did not want to miss any school, I took my mother's advice and put a scarf on my head thinking that the walk to school (yes we walked – both ways!) would flatten my "big hair."

When I arrived at school, my hair was just as horrible, if not worse! I brushed it continually, trying to help the situation. I held my hand to my head and tried to avoid some of my other eighth grade classmates.

To my dismay, we were all called down to the school nurse's office to get our height and weight taken that day. While waiting in line by the office, I was spotted by an African-American boy named Alonzo who was the class clown. Although I always liked him, I was now trying to hide from him. In his customary way, he seized the opportunity. He looked at me intently, smirked, and said, "Now, you are one of us!"

I really do not remember what my exact reply was, but I do recall laughing with him and the few other students who were also on line. The laughter broke the tension, and I was then able to explain the situation briefly without anyone's feelings being hurt. I felt much better. I had gotten a well-deserved reprieve. After school, I went home and was able to wash and set my hair that night. When I came into school the next day, I looked a lot more like me!

As an adult, and as a seventh and eighth grade teacher for most of my teaching career, I also used humor sometimes as a way of handling difficult situations to counter what could have possibly led to hurt feelings and tears if I had not.

I particularly remember two situations which, I think, exemplify how the use of humor can help you get through a tough time.

Due to personal circumstances, there was a gap of a few years in my full-time classroom teaching. Fortunately, when my son had just entered the first grade, an opening to teach in a local middle school presented itself. The position involved my taking over an eighth grade class for a teacher who could not handle the students from a classroom management point of view. I became the temporary, full-time eighth grade social studies teacher in October and stayed until the school year ended in June. With the firm resolve to be a success in this endeavor, and the necessary support from a wonderful team of teachers, I looked at this opportunity as a challenge with which to begin the second phase of my teaching career.

In order to get the upper hand in this difficult situation, I used my firm, fair and consistent approach, which had been the foundation of all my teaching and classroom management. Slowly but surely, I was able to get the social studies classes under control and get learning back on track again. The classroom environment was now both safe (physically and emotionally) and productive. The "fun" part in learning could now begin.

The first situation happened in the late winter. I had set up a record player on my desk in the front of the room. As I was introducing the lesson, I "gracefully" tripped over the record player's electric cord and landed on my both knees behind my desk – disappearing from the students' view.

As I was getting over my embarrassment at having tripped and fallen, I began to get up, and I peered over the top of my desk. The classroom was so quiet that you could have heard a pin drop. In trying to make a quick comeback and release the tension I now sensed, I told the class, "Now you can say that your teacher went down in history!"

Everyone, including me, had a good laugh, and I was able to restore order quickly. My use of comedic wordplay, my "humanness," and the students' reaction in this situation, proved to me that a real bonding was taking place.

In the late spring of that same year, I entered the same classroom in which I had tripped and fallen. While I was walking in, I overheard a few students talking quietly and I heard one say, "Let's get to 'Sarge's' class." I thought to myself that this must be a reference to my strictness in class and the "tight ship" I had run because of the circumstances under which I had become their teacher.

After the class settled in, but before I introduced the lesson, I made a brief reference to the pre-class conversation I had overheard and thanked those responsible for having referred to me as "Sarge." I quickly added, "By the end of the year, I expect to be promoted to General!" The class, and I, laughed. But again, all was quiet within a few moments, and the class lesson got underway.

In both of these situations, humor not only saved the day, but it also added a human element. At the end of the school year, I received several personal notes and comments from students and parents thanking me for the great school year that they had. I still have their class picture in my scrapbook!

LESSON - Use humor, when appropriate, and learn to be able to laugh at yourself! By doing so, you can possibly divert a more serious or negative outcome and prove to yourself and others that you are human!

Chapter 9

Understanding the Mind-Body Connection

IF YOU ARE to be a truly effective person in your life, your observations must be constant and proactive.

I will never forget a particular day in the mid-1990's. It was the first day of school and I was walking with my class from my homeroom to the gym for a welcoming greeting from the principal. Looking at the group of twenty or so students, I had a feeling of excitement for the upcoming year. At that moment, I observed a new student; and, just by looking in his eyes, which appeared to be glazed, I knew that something was wrong. His body movements matched that glaze and after just a few moments, I realized that something was terribly amiss, so I got him to the school nurse immediately. Just after he got into the nurse's office, he fainted! After the school nurse examined the young boy and he had a chance to rest for a while, he was allowed to go home. The next day, his mother called me to thank me for my keen perception and follow-through.

Being careful to watch everything that is going on with your students is important. You should be alert to any changes in "normal" behavior or other indications that something might not be right with a student. When your students are with you, they are your "children" and are in your living room (the classroom)! It is your responsibility to create a safe environment for them. Emotions and feelings go far beyond someone not hurting, or allowing someone to hurt another's heart. You are dealing with physical as well as emotional issues, and your "atuneness" to them must be working at its maximum at all times.

Even today, I remember the secure and caring feeling some of my teachers gave me especially when my physical health was concerned.

SCHOOLTIME REFLECTIONS - FEELINGS 202

My fifth grade teacher sat beside me on bus trips because she knew I suffered from motion sickness. My ninth grade teacher asked the school nurse to climb three flights of stairs to see me rather than have me, with broken and dislocated toes, climb the stairs both ways to her office!

These two incidents touched my heart and left me with warm feelings. These teachers were true nurturers and really cared. As a result, I felt secure both physically and emotionally.

<u>LESSON</u> - A holistic approach toward emotions and feelings is essential to show students that you genuinely care about their physical and emotional well-being.

Chapter 10

Using Names Correctly

NAMES, YOUR DISTINCTIVE nomenclature, are an important part of everyone's identity and, therefore, should be used correctly. They should also be spelled and pronounced correctly! This is very significant, as each person is unique in this universe and should be respected.

As teachers, we have an obligation to know our students' names. Having suffered "name abuse" throughout my life, I have made this a priority in my teaching career.

A brief history: Beginning in kindergarten, my name was misspelled and mispronounced. My full name is Margaret Mary Dunajski. My nickname is Margie (and my married name is Harde). My name was rarely used correctly, spelled correctly, or pronounced correctly throughout my student life or my teaching career. I was incorrectly called Marjorie or Marge. Both of which bothered me. Marjorie reminded me of margarine, which was that orange-colored and terrible-tasting bread spread that was used in the late 1940's. Marge reminded me of a waitress in a comedy sitcom on T.V. Not that I have anything against waitresses, but I had an unhappy and stressful experience as a waitress one summer at a restaurant in Lake George, New York, during my college years (the owner even said that I would have made a better hostess)!

My last name, Dunajski, was also mispronounced miserably. When I started to teach, I used to write my name on the blackboard phonetically, spell it correctly, and then take the time to pronounce it correctly to the class: Miss Dunajski – and phonetically – Da-nice-ski. The students called me Miss Dunajski when I was single and Mrs. Harde (Har-dee) after I was married. Because of my first day introductions and my insistence on correct usage, they pronounced both of my names beautifully.

SCHOOLTIME REFLECTIONS - FEELINGS 202

I also made a genuine, ongoing effort to pronounce and spell correctly the names of the more than one hundred students I had in class each year. I encouraged them to correct me if I made an error, no matter when, and, unlike myself, not to accept their name being misspelled or mispronounced.

I also know that people sometimes get a little out of sorts if you try to correct them, even if it is constructive. However, by the same token, they expect that their names will be used correctly. Furthermore, people sometimes do not seem to care about this unless it affects them directly. It seems to be a very selfish approach.

This one-sided and thoughtless attitude was clearly exemplified as when my son, Karl, experienced a totally incorrect use of his name. On the first day of school, as his first grade teacher was taking attendance, she called Karl's name out as "Stanley." He attempted politely to correct the teacher and tell her that his first name was Karl, and that Stanley was his middle name. But, in response, she came back by saying," That is what is printed on my list – that is what it is – so I will have to check…!" What kind of a response was that to give a young student? Karl was not even six years old at the time and he must have felt crushed.

Just after the teacher made her comment about the attendance list, another student in the class, who knew Karl, showed his support by exclaiming to the teacher that my son's name was really Karl! I am sure that the friend's loyalty touched my son's heart and was able to soften the teacher's inappropriate remarks and the mistake.

Even though Karl's teacher probably found out by the next morning that the attendance list was printed incorrectly, having Stanley instead of Karl for my son's first name, she never made any attempt to apologize to him for the error, or how she handled the situation. My son and I still remember this incident and how it demonstrates the importance of using names correctly.

Names – Please be more empathetic to people's feelings when it comes to labeling with names. This sensitivity about names has an umbrella effect. Names become a part of you in any culture. Some interesting and fun-filled teaching and learning experiences about this follow:

SCHOOLTIME REFLECTIONS - FEELINGS 202

When I taught a social studies class a unit about Native Americans, we had a naming day. I placed the students into cooperative groups based upon the five tribes of the New York State Iroquois Confederacy Indians (Ex. Mohawk tribe). Once in a group, each student was to be given a tribal name. They were to come up with their Native American tribal names based upon their own personalities and/or appearances and nature. My students named me "Princess Rainbow," and I kept and always used that name.

As an aside, I was given the name beginning with "Princess" because of its connection with a lesson I had taught them previously in a social studies unit about the five boroughs that make up New York City. I used a "true" gimmick, based upon my life, to help them remember each borough. I would say, "My mother was born in Queens County (Blissville, Long Island City) and my father was born in Kings County (Williamsburg, Brooklyn) - and so, a 'king' married a 'queen' and after they moved to Peekskill, they had a 'princess'!" I would then do a curtsey! After that, they always remembered that Brooklyn was called Kings County, etc! I also used this technique later on when I taught a unit on Exploration by adding that the "princess" married Prince Henry (my husband's name) the

Navigator! By adapting this easy instructional technique, the students had "fun" remembering these historical and geographical bits of information.

In the Native-American Unit, the students would think carefully and then give themselves names that they thought fit the criteria and of which they could be proud. To name a few: "Creative Frog" was a good name for a talented artist who had a frog for a pet; "Slow Turtle" was always late for class and liked turtles; "Dancing Star" loved to dance and had a "sparkling personality"! Even some of the other teachers joined in - "Tall Oak" was the name taken by a tall and handsome physical education teacher. "Sensitive Wolf" was taken by another teacher who was kind and caring about others as well as being dapper! By the time I retired from full-time teaching, I even had "Native American" names (I helped name some) for most of the faculty!

> LESSON - Names are as special and as important as the people they represent. Teachers, please use, spell, and pronounce your students' (and other people's) names accurately. It is really a matter of genuine respect and caring of a human right. We are only here once and we should be addressed and remembered properly.

CHAPTER 11

Discovering When Feelings Begin

FEELINGS, SENSITIVITY, INSTINCTS, or emotions, although they sometimes appear to be short-lived, seem to stay with us for a long time and can become a part of our inner fiber.

I have tried to reinforce kind and gentle ways when dealing with life's heart-sensitive issues with everyone. The development of these two qualities is important in ourselves if we are to consider the feelings of others while being true to ourselves. This fact was never more pronounced as when each of my "grandtwins" said things that really brought to light how important feelings are from a very early age. I would like to highlight a few experiences I had with them before they entered preschool.

Kayla Margaret, whom I nicknamed "Kurlycue," once took two small pieces of paper, taped them together, and wrote on the "cover," "*Nana's Book.*" On the inside, she drew a happy-face stick person on one side of the paper and a sad-face stick figure on the other side. I asked her why her second stick figure was sad. She explained, "Someone hurt her feelings!" Naturally, this experience culminated with a great big embrace and tender hand-holding. The holding of my hand or finger(s), I believe, has given my granddaughter a sense of happiness and Nana-type loving and security since the day she was born. On that day, very soon after coming into the Natal Intensive Care Unit, my husband and I went in to see her. I went over to Kayla's incubator, reached over, and touched her hand. Her little fingers wrapped around my little finger (pinky) and she just held on! My husband, Kayla's Papa, saw the glow of pure "Nana-hood" in my eyes the moment she touched me. The glow remains!

Soon after coming home from the hospital, Papa and I went with the twins and their mother on a scheduled visit to the pediatrician's office. While the doctor was examining her twin brother, Zachary, Kayla became distressed and started to cry. To comfort her, I extended my hand, which she grabbed and began to stroke. The result was that she stopped crying and calmed down until it was her turn to be examined by the doctor.

The reassuring feeling that we shared was also exemplified on a Friday when I was babysitting for my "grandtwins" on "Fridays with Nana." A physical therapist had been coming to the house and was working with Kayla. On this particular day, Kayla was visibly upset as she tried to walk toward the therapist. At the direction of the therapist, I extended my arms. Kayla smiled and took some steps toward me into my open arms. This calming experience and feeling of security has continued in the holding of our hands and "hearts" when we are together.

Zachary also wears his "heart" on his sleeve. When Zachary, whom I nicknamed "Star," was three and a half years old, he sang "Happy Birthday" to me and then "Happy Marriage" to my husband and me to the tune of "Happy Birthday." He gave us a toy birthday cake. It was actually his "Papa's" and my twenty-fifth wedding anniversary in about four days, and he wanted to sing to us. I told him that he was always kind – and never hurt

Nana's feelings. He looked up at me and said, "Only bad people hurt your heart!" We then looked into each other's eyes, and he kissed me very tenderly. Zachary showed this sensitivity again one Halloween evening as I followed my "grandtwins" and their parents on a "Trick or Treat" outing. He turned around on several occasions and asked, "Are you safe, Nana?" The compassion and caring Zachary displayed by his kind actions and words, and his protective nature, continue to be an integral part of his personality.

As you observe the facial expressions and listen to the sounds of babies and young children, they will tell you whether they are afraid, happy, upset, etc. We all seem to take that for granted as a part of their temperament. However, if we linger a while longer with the expression's impact and importance, we can really see how essential feelings really are, right from the beginnings of life. Moreover, we can reinforce this young empathy as we watch our children and grandchildren grow.

LESSON - Never underestimate when feelings begin in young lives. Feelings are at the "heart" of our very existence. They begin when life begins.

Chapter 12

Keeping in Mind the Importance of Feelings and Your Career

THROUGH ALL OF my early school experiences, both emotionally positive and negative, I always knew that I wanted to become a teacher. I believe that the idea and feelings were there from the day I was born. As a teacher, I could touch young peoples' lives, be a leader, be respected, and leave my mark. Oh, how blessed I was to know the path to take to my career.

Although there were several other occasions I could have written about where certain teachers could have used a beginning course or even "refresher" course on sensitivity, I want to conclude on a truly positive personal note and focus on a time when I felt I was most impressionable.

In my ninth grade, one of my teachers, along with the foundation of constant love and support I received from my parents, became a real springboard for my life's career.

The idea of becoming a teacher in the field of social studies was really nurtured while I attended the former Drum Hill Jr. High School in Peekskill, NY. I was truly inspired to pursue this career goal by Mr. Ed Jacobson, one of my ninth grade teachers. Since I have been using the alphabet in order to put a "name" to each of the teachers I have discussed, it is ironic that the next letter to identify this teacher would have been "J".

I encountered Mr. Jacobson in two academic subjects – social studies and English, and in one extracurricular activity – our school newspaper. I grew to admire him as a teacher and as a person. I will never forget the lasting impression that he made on me during my adolescence. I was amazed by how he inspired students to think and to take pride in their work. He helped me to learn how to think on my own and to enter onto paths of knowledge I never knew existed. I realized in his class that social studies took in aspects of many curriculums (interdisciplinary) and it was really the study of people. What could be more interesting? Mr. Jacobson held out high expectations for all of his students and was, therefore, demanding, challenging, sympathetic, creative, and a true motivator. In another bit of irony, he was later to become my principal when I was hired as a seventh grade social studies teacher in that same school, Drum Hill Junior High School.

My dreams were fine-tuned when I decided that teaching young adolescents would be the path I would take. Although I enjoy teaching at all age levels, I have found that the middle-school age child is the most challenging. And besides, somebody has to love them!

So many important changes take place in young peoples' lives during their middle school years. To use an analogy I have shared with students, parents and others over the years, I believe that when young teenagers enter this phase in their maturation, they are in "cocoons." When they go on to the next phase in their maturation, they will have either grown to become "moths" or "butterflies," depending upon the many factors which have influenced their development. During their maturation process, they will experience many of the "firsts" in their lives in the process of learning about themselves as they pass through these formative and character-developing years. At all ages, once a child builds his/her positive self-esteem and once he/she believes in him/her self, that child will learn that they can succeed, not only in school – but also more importantly – in life!

> <u>LESSON</u> - Feelings, it is all about feelings. Examining and understanding your feelings should help you in making satisfying career choices. Since emotions are at the heart of life, I always told my students, "love what you do!"

Chapter 13

Concluding Observations and Summary

THE REAL-LIFE STORIES described in the previous chapters helped me to develop the "lessons" presented. In addition to these "lessons" helping me to understand and deal with students during my teaching career, I have been able to apply them in other aspects of my life as well. They have really served as positive, proactive emotional guides.

In summarizing these "lessons," I suggest that there are five important points for you to remember:

1. When you "touch" or impact your students' lives in a genuine way, you will remain in their hearts forever.
2. Put yourself in your students' place and you will be in a better position to feel a true empathy. Be observant and take the time to look into their eyes, minds, and hearts. Use a holistic approach and even include humor, when appropriate, and you will help to build their self-esteem.
3. Respect has to be earned and it is always a two-way street. Do not talk down to students or underestimate their situations or their concerns.
4. Be firm, fair, and consistent in your disciplinary approach and your students' respect for you will grow. This approach can also have a major impact on the way they develop their relationships with others. Naturally, this should be coupled with your emotional insight. In addition, when your teaching environment is safe, positive, and productive, you will all have "fun" learning.
5. If you slip and make a mistake or if you are inappropriate or use a caustic tone in dealing with a student's feelings or concerns, be genuine, and say, "I'm sorry," to

them. Forgiveness is a necessary part of all meaningful relationships.

Remember that introspective intellect makes good teachers. This, together with true compassion for others and a passion for your life's career, makes the best teachers in and out of school. What it comes down to is that life is really all about one's emotions and true feelings. The one constant that affects every aspect of our lives, the heart of life itself, and - the one with which we are born and with which we leave this world - is OUR FEELINGS.